"DELIVER US FROM EVIL"

By Apostle Stephen A. Garner

RIVERS PUBLISHING COMPANY
CHICAGO, IL

DELIVER US FROM EVIL
Copyright ©2011 Stephen A. Garner
P.O. Box 1545
Bolingbrook, IL 60440

Cover Design by Rivers Publishing Company

Published by Rivers Publishing Company

All rights reserved. No portion of this book may be reproduced, scanned, or stored in a retrieval system, transmitted in any form or by any means – electronic, mechanical, photocopy, recording, or any other – except for brief quotations in printed reviews without written permission of the publisher. Please do not participate in or encourage piracy of copyrighted materials in violation of the author's rights. Purchase only authorized editions.

Unless otherwise indicated, all scriptural quotations are taken from the *King James Version* of the Holy Bible. All Hebraic and Greek definitions are taken from the *Strong's Exhaustive Concordance*, Baker Book House: Grand Rapids, Michigan

Rivers Publishing Company
Stephen A. Garner Ministries
P.O. Box 1545, Bolingbrook, IL 60440
E-mail: sagarnerministries@gmail.com
www.sagministries.com

ISBN 978-0-9844783-8-5

Printed in the United States of America

Table of Contents

Foreword   3

Chapter 1
Deliver Us From Evil   5

Chapter 2
Old Testament Examples of Evil   10

Chapter 3
New Testament Types of Evil   28

Chapter 4
The Root of All Evil   40

Foreword

Deliver Us From Evil is a practical book that gives understanding into the origin and progression of evil with insights taken from both the Old and New Testaments of the Bible. Apostle Stephen Garner does a great job of bringing practical and relevant information into this important subject.

He states that, "Liberating people is far more difficult than leading them." This is because many leaders do not understand the underlying systems of evil that are in operation, which have not been broken through deliverance, that continue to work in the lives of those they lead. In this powerful publication you learn the various ways in which evil manifests and how to gain victory over them.

Apostle Garner makes it clear that believers, who have come out of lifestyles where lewdness and sexual immorality were the norm, are in need of deliverance from the spirit of Belial. In this practical and easy read book, you will gain comprehension of what the spirit of Belial is, and other definitions of biblical terms that are associated with the manifestation of evil.

The mantle of intercession and deliverance that is upon Apostle Garner brings him to the cutting edge of Kingdom issues, providing solutions that will bring deliverance to those who are held captive by the forces of evil. This liberation will be the catalyst that will result in Kingdom Advancement, because when an individual is set free, he can then be used effectively by God to do the work of the ministry.

Be blessed as you explore the pages of this book of fresh revelation. May your heart and minds be purged from any residue of Belial that may be lurking in the shadows of your existence.

Apostle Lorenzo Irving
Life Center Church of Deliverance
Chicago, IL

CHAPTER 1

DELIVER US FROM EVIL

DELIVER US FROM EVIL

*"And lead us not into temptation;
but deliver us from evil"*
Luke 11:4b

This is a very powerful passage of scripture which I've quoted for years during times of prayer. I've also used this verse when teaching on intercession as it relates to spiritual warfare. My position has been, if evil isn't an issue for the believer then Christ would have never given instructions to pray for deliverance from it. The Lord provides proper insight on how the believer is to deal with evil; cry unto Him for deliverance from its influence and its effects. Evil is defined as profoundly immoral or wrong, an act which causes harm, pain or injustice. Something very unpleasant as it relates to the devil or other destructive forces, evil spirits.

There are several ways for evil to manifest in or against a person. The Lord says in **Matthew 5:11 *"Blessed are ye, when men shall revile you and persecute you and shall say all manner of evil against you falsely, for my sake."*** Evil, in this case, can be spoken or pronounced over/against a person's life. Many people have found themselves ensnared by words they've spoken or the words of others. The Lord declares the words which He speaks are spirit and life. He was God manifested in the flesh. He knew no sin and therefore He could only speak truth and release life. We on the other hand are prone to say and do things in error, releasing evil and destruction. King David asked God to set a watch at his mouth and keep the door of his lips. Profanity, gossip, slander, accusations, murmuring, complaining and lies are all released through words and spirits of destruction come along with them. This is why we must let our speech be always with grace, seasoned with salt, that we may know how we ought to answer every man. Colossians 4:6

Matthew 6:22-23 "The light of the body is the eye: if therefore thine eye be single, thy whole body shall be full of light. But if thine eye be evil, thy whole body shall be full of darkness. If therefore the light that is in thee be darkness, how great is that darkness." The light or thing which illuminates the body is the eye and if our eye is single or clear, our entire life is illuminated with God's goodness. However, on the other hand, evil or an evil eye has the capacity to corrupt our entire lives with darkness which speaks of obscurity or shadiness. Our vision is directly connected to our perception, both naturally and spiritually. Many people struggle today with distortions in their perception. I've dealt with numerous situations where believers have felt ill-treated or indifferent about other believers because of shadiness or obscurity rooted in the evil eye. This manifestation of evil has caused many God ordained relationships to be destroyed. If we lack the capacity to do well despite what we see in others, we could be dealing with an evil eye and in need of deliverance.

Matthew 7:20 "Wherefore by their fruits shall ye know them" and Matthew 7:23 "And then will I profess unto them, I never knew you: depart from, ye that work iniquity." The fruit of our life is directly connected to our value systems. Many have declared themselves to be one way or another, but lack or have any abundance of fruit to validate what they say. This is probably one of the most noticeable ways of evil manifesting. The Lord says we're known by our fruit and that many who have done works in His name shall be informed by Him that He never knew them because of iniquity. The fruit which we bring forth is the determining factor as to evil or righteousness. The Lord says a good tree brings forth good fruit and a corrupt tree evil fruit. Righteousness is of God and He that works righteousness is of God. Gifts and callings don't validate a persons' righteousness, only Christ. People can function in Christ-ordained works and be influenced by evil in both their deeds and nature. The gifts are irrevocable and don't require a repentant lifestyle in order to work. Let us therefore be not overcome with evil, but rather overcome evil by doing good.

> *People can function in Christ-ordained works and be influenced by evil in both their deeds and nature.*

Let's take a deeper look at the nature of evil by highlighting some examples from the Old & New Testament. If we're to effectively overcome and walk delivered from evil, we need a good "Word" regiment to help us discern what's declared evil. Christ has assured us of ultimate victory against evil and deliverance from it because of the work He fulfilled on the cross.

Chapter 2

Old Testament Examples of Evil

OLD TESTAMENT EXAMPLES OF EVIL

"And out of the ground made the Lord God to grow every tree that is pleasant to sight and good for food; the tree of life also in the midst of the garden, and the tree of knowledge of good and evil."
Genesis 2:9

"And the Lord God commanded the man, saying, of every tree of the garden thou mayest freely eat: but of the tree of the knowledge of good and evil, thou shalt not eat of it: for in the day that thou eatest thereof thou shalt surely die."
Genesis 2:16-17

Let's explore a few Old Testament words for evil. There are several Hebrew words which we will use to help develop this study. The Hebrew reference keys are provided for further examination; and to fortify our understanding concerning the nature of evil.

One way to develop a healthy biblical word study is to find the first time a word is mentioned, determine what subject(s) are addressed in the context of the verse(s), and then look for examples or references of that word and its meaning in other passages of scripture. This is known as the law of first mention or the law of first reference. It helps to establish consistency of thoughts and subjects we teach on words, evil in this case.

Evil in the referenced verses is the Hebrew word *"Ra"* found in key H7451 which means adversity, affliction, bad, calamity, distress, ill-favored, exceedingly grievous, sorrow, wretchedness, misery and naught. This kind of evil is often connected to **choices we make** contrary to God's word and His purpose for our lives. We were designed by God with the power of choice. God knew that man would transgress and fall short of obeying His words. However, He provided a plan of redemption which has been fulfilled in Christ. Adam and Eve ate from the tree of knowledge of good and evil, a choice which opened them and the entire human race to the adversity, affliction, sorrow and wretchedness of sin. Genesis chapters 3-4 show the progression of sorrow and pain Adam & Eve had to live with because of evil.

There are many people today who are reaping all sorts of calamity, distress, adversity and afflictions due to the influence of evil. Choices made, such as bad business decisions or ill-advised counsel concerning relationships. People are finding themselves on the brink of utter ruin. There are many causes we can attribute to this. For example, lack of wisdom, education and keeping company with the wrong people can lead to poor choices, which open doors to calamity, adversity and affliction. Lack of patience or lack of research, wrong motive(s) and pressure because time restraints could also be on the list. God has equally given all of us the power of choice. How we utilize this power often determines the outcome of our lives. I admonish you to choose wisely.

When we make decisions to act apart from the counsel of God's word, evil will prevail against us and often those we are in relationships with. Just as in the case with Adam and Eve, there was a rippling effect impacting generations because of their disobedience to God. A door was opened for the entrance of evil into the human race and we're still dealing with the ramifications today. We too can see in our personal lives or those we know on a personal level the damage done to the innocent because of bad choices.

Lord, deliver me from evil...

"Father in the name of Jesus I come out of agreement with all rippling effects of evil loosed against me because of poor choices and ill-advised decisions I've made. I renounce all assignments of evil programs against my life because of bad decisions made by those who have preceded me. I decree I am free from every generational effect of wickedness. I pronounce over my life a walk free from all calamity, distress, adversity, afflictions, sorrow, grief and wretchedness because you nailed them all to the cross and you died for me and rose again from the dead that I may have abundance of life in the name of Jesus!"

"And Moses returned unto the Lord, and said, Lord, wherefore has thou so evil entreated this people? Why is it that thou hast sent me? For since I came to Pharaoh to speak in thy name, he hath done evil to this people; neither has thou delivered thy people at all."

Exodus 5:22-23

The word evil in these verses come from the Hebrew word **"Raw-ah"** found in key H7489 which means to spoil literally by breaking to pieces, to make or cause to be good for nothing, to make bad from a physical, moral and social aspect, to afflict. This kind of evil is rooted in **harsh mistreatment** by oppressors who show no mercy and sometimes will cause the believer to blame God and those whom He sends to lead us.

> *I have found in ministry that liberating God's people is far more difficult than leading them.*

The prophet Moses had the challenging task of liberating Israel from Egypt physically, but the damaging effects on them psychologically from slavery and bondage would prove to be a very challenging and an even more difficult task. The 435 years of captivity had broken down the morale of God's people to the point where many found it more pleasing to remain in captivity than to go through the process of redemption which would lead to their freedom.

I have found in ministry that liberating God's people is far more difficult than leading them. People, who come out of abusive and controlling lifestyles, find it very difficult to trust. They find it even more difficult to yield and submit to righteous leadership ordained to bless. This could be the result of harsh mistreatment they have gone through, where they've been broken to pieces mentally and/or emotionally because of evil.

Just like in the case of Moses where Pharaoh increased bondage against the people of God, there are certain spirits at work in individuals that will not let them mentally and/or emotionally receive freedom. They are left to feel unworthy. It's almost like trying to leave a relationship and the person you are separating from refuses to let you go and he/she continues to remind you of how bad you are in order to maintain control. Demons often will operate in this manner especially among those who suffer from rejection and self-esteem issues. Thanks be unto God however, who has redeemed us through the shed blood of Jesus Christ. His blood also has a voice and it speaks better things than the voice of oppressive spirits assigned to destroy us.

Lord, deliver me from evil...

"I come out of agreement with all programs, assignments of bondage, control, slavery and oppression. I proclaim liberation from every declaration of Pharaoh in my blood line. Spirits that seek to minimize and cut off deliverance in my life. I renounce all devils that seek to lock me into mindsets and meditations contrary to God's word concerning me as His beloved. I decree a release from your plots, schemes and secret agendas at work to restrict breakthrough and momentum in my life. I decree I am significant in the plan of God and I claim this in the mighty name of Jesus!"

"And the Lord spake unto Moses, saying, send out men, that they may search the land of Canaan, which I give unto the children of Israel: of every tribe of their fathers shall ye send man, everyone a ruler among. And Moses by the commandment of the Lord sent them from the wilderness of Paran: all those men were the heads of the children of Israel."
Numbers 13:1-3

"And they brought up an evil report of the land which they had searched unto the children of Israel, saying, the land, through which we have gone to search it, is a land that eateth up the inhabitants thereof; and all the people we saw in it are men of great stature."
Numbers 13:32

In this age of technological advancements, the capacity of mass media has increased tremendously. Events taking place in remote parts of the world are often streamed immediately before the masses. Along with this increase of capacity to reveal vital information in order for life to be preserved or sustained, the opportunity to spread evil reports is just as potent. The children of Israel under the leadership of Moses faced a situation where evil reports caused the nation to be changed forever.

They were in a season of advancement and the evil influences of Egyptian captivity proved to be fatal to the generation God had delivered. Their fear of the giants in the land led them to bring Moses an evil report. There are people in every level of society for one reason or another, because of fear, fail to give accurate reports.

Numbers 13:17 –20 gives us a detailed insight into what the men were to report on. They were to see the land, the people who were dwelling there and report whether they were strong or weak. They were also to report how many were dwelling in the land. They were to give a report whether the land was good or bad and whether the cities could be inhabited. They were also to report concerning whether the land was fat or lean. Moses charged them prior to sending them out to be of good courage and bring back fruit of the land. The men failed this test miserably apart from the testimony of Caleb and Joshua. Unfortunately, the agenda of Satan was accomplished once the report of evil was released. An entire generation of covenant people, delivered by the power of God from bondage in Egypt, all died before they entered the promise land as ordained by God.

This kind of evil in the referenced verse comes from two root words found in keys *H1680* **Daw-bab** *and H1679* **Do-beh** which means to move slowly, to glide, to cause to speak, to be sluggish, that is restful. There are times when tremendous amounts of spiritual momentum can be gained by individuals and congregations alike, however, one evil report can cause

Spirit-ordained works to become sluggish and slow moving.

The Lord admonishes us in Mark 4:24 to take heed what ye hear and in Luke 8:18 to take heed therefore how ye hear. What and how we hear often effects how we respond. For example the ten spies, who returned an evil report, caused the generation which came out of Egypt to slowly glide away from their original assignment and ultimately die without inheriting the promise. Of course Joshua and Caleb had another spirit and their generation continued in gaining momentum because they returned with a good report which synchronized with the plan of God.

Gifted people and gifted congregations are to be especially aware of how they hear and what they hear. Have you ever received information, contrary to what you know to be true based upon the word of God, and you chose out of fear to go against the prompting of the Holy Spirit? This is exactly what happened to those spies sent by Moses with specific instructions as to what they were to report on. They were moved by what they saw instead of being moved by what they were instructed to do and eventually their transition from bondage to promise came to an abrupt ending. There are life lessons to be learned from this referenced account. As you meditate upon God's plan for your life, I trust that faith will arise in you and evil reports which will come, shall have no effect upon your obedience and pursuit of his promise.

Lord, deliver me from evil...

"Father in the name of Jesus I decree my ears are circumcised from the impact and influence of evil reports. I will not glide nor stray away from what you've ordained for my life. I receive every promise as yes and amen. Lord open my eyes to see the fruit of the land of promise for me and let me not be moved by the giants that stand in the way. For with you all things are possible to them that believe."

The name of Belial is found in key *H1100* **Bel-e-yah-al** and mentioned sixteen times throughout the Bible. It is a word which is used to describe individuals that represent the lowest level of life. All of the references, with the exception of one, are found in the Old Testament. This name was often associated with men who operated in some of the most depraved and morally vile behavior imaginable. There are accounts of bearing false witness, murder, sexual lewdness, idolatry and a host of other works which shouldn't be named among covenant people.

Belial is also synonymous with the type of evil which literally means without profit, worthlessness, by ext., destruction, wickedness as it relates to ungodly men and naughtiness. This kind of evil leads individuals to lawlessness and disdain for the righteousness of God.

"Certain men, the children of Belial, are gone out from among you and have withdrawn the inhabitants of their city, saying, let us go and serve other gods."

Deuteronomy 13:13

Evil, associated with the children of Belial, can be visibly seen in those who seduce the innocent into transgressing against God by serving idols. Idolatry, which is forbidden by God, is an evil practice used by the children of Belial to draw believer's evil practices. We are to be especially aware of seductive powers bent on leading us astray from the truth into idolatrous worship. Remember one of the aims of this kind of evil is to get us engaged in worthlessness that will lead to our destruction. I John 5:21 admonishes us to keep ourselves from idols. We are to guard ourselves and be watchful concerning idolatry.

Judges chapters 19-20 provides insight into the levels of depravity the sons of Belial indulge in. There was a certain Levite who was traveling along with his concubine. She left him and remained at large for several months. The Levite locates her and goes to redeem his wife according to Judges 19:3. The Levite then departs from his father-in-law's home several days later.

As the story progresses, the Levite and his concubine enter a city where the sons of Belial abide. A man of that city takes the Levite and his concubine in. The sons of Belial come to the man's home and demand sex from the Levite. This speaks to the levels of lawlessness and lewdness that the children of Belial operate in. The man of the city, who took the Levite in, offered them his daughter but they insisted on having the man. The fact that this man would offer them his daughter shows how the presence of the Belial kind of evil causes moral decay territorially.

We can see this in regions today where vileness and sexual immorality are running rampant. For instance, pilgrims who participate in Mardi Gras are overcome with the spirit of the region where the festival is held. This is also true of the Carnivale which is held in

Trinidad and Brazil. The activities of these festivals are full of worthless deeds rooted in vileness.

Some of the demons that work with Belial are spirits of rape, incest, sexual abuse, uncleanness, filthiness, sodomy and obscenity to name a few. Eventually they took the Levite's concubine and defiled her all night. The next morning she was found at the door of the house dead where the Levite settled. He then takes her body cuts it into 12 pieces and distributes it throughout the tribes of Israel. This speaks to even more depravity and as a result of this wickedness thousands of the Benjamites were destroyed of whom were the sons of Belial.

> *Some of the demons that work with Belial are spirits of rape, incest, sexual abuse, uncleanness, filthiness, sodomy and obscenity to name a few.*

Believers who have come out of lifestyles where lewdness and sexual immorality were the norm for them are in need of deliverance from the spirit of Belial. Counseling for emotional and psychological issues should be encouraged as well. Some of the demons that work with Belial are spirits of rape, incest, sexual abuse, uncleanness, filthiness, sodomy and obscenity to name a few. This brief glimpse of the Belial type of evil highlights the declaration of the Lord from Luke 11:4b, where we are admonished to cry unto Him for deliverance from evil.

One final example of the Belial type evil is found in I Kings 21. This is an account where a righteous man named Naboth was murdered because he refused to part with his family's inheritance at the request of King Ahab. Jezebel, Ahab's wife, arose and used the sons of Belial to conspire against Naboth. I Kings 21:9-16 shows how this scheme was fulfilled and the role of evil executed by Jezebel and the sons of Belial. Remember this type of evil leads people into worthless and destructive deeds.

Lord, deliver me from evil…

"Arise Lord as my helper and my defender against all assignments of worthlessness, immorality, uncleanness and vileness rooted in the spirit of Belial. I renounce all manifestations connected with drunkenness, Jezebel, idolatry and murder. I rebuke all lust, perversion and sexual uncleanness known and unknown associated with my thoughts, my family line or from past relationship. I declare a baptism of holiness is my portion in Jesus Name!"

CHAPTER 3

NEW TESTAMENT TYPES OF EVIL

NEW TESTAMENT TYPES OF EVIL

In this section we will briefly look at three Greek words used for evil and their reference keys for further study of this subject. First I want you to take special note of the relationship between evil and the words we speak. Proverbs 18:21 states, "Death and life are in the power of the tongue: and they that love it shall eat the fruit thereof." Our words are powerful and have the capacity to shape our future for good or bad. Many people today are reaping fruit from things spoken over them to their detriment or success.

> *This is why spirit-filled counselors are needed in ministry today.*

Secondly, note the physical and/or emotional impact that evil produces on an individual. There are many people who live injured internally and the diagnosis has been made from an external point of view only. Sometimes the root cause of toxic or unwholesome behavior has a lot to do with the work of evil eating away at an individual's soul like a cancer. This is why spirit-filled counselors are needed in ministry today. Jesus had the spirit of counsel on his life and the Body of Christ is in desperate need of it today. God desires that we move beyond surface healing and embrace removal of root systems.

The last aspect of evil we will cover is that which is rooted in corruption. There is a driving force that is common to the human race because of sin which distorts integrity. Some people are just corrupt on purpose. They know that their actions are illegal, yet they feel that's just the way they are and find a measure of comfort being evil. Then there are others who because of circumstances and poor value systems embrace desires and passions they know are wrong. This is often the case when self-gratification is the issue, resulting in someone else's demise. We have witnessed this to be all too common in our communities. Where spiritual leaders, political leaders, financial advisors and business people alike pursue their selfish desires and leave those they represent slighted.

"But those things which proceed out of the mouth come forth from the heart; and they defile the man. For out of the heart proceed evil thoughts, murders, adulteries, fornications, thefts, false witnesses, blasphemies: These are the things which defile a man: but to eat with unwashen hands defileth not a man."

Matthew 15:19-20

Jesus is providing revelation concerning the source of man's defilement. His religious contemporaries were making an issue out of his disciples not washing their hands before eating. We know this to be a sanitary issue, but the Lord was providing insight into a spiritual sanitary issue, the wickedness of man's heart.

Scripture tells us that the heart of man above all is deceitful and desperately wicked and God knows this. Religion will often focus on the external, but the Lord tries our hearts. In this instance, the defilement Jesus speaks of deals with the words that come out of the mouth and the source of those words being man's heart.

> *This kind of evil normally results in severe damage being inflicted on others through our words.*

Verse 19 shows us that from the heart proceeds evil thoughts along with several other things. The word evil in this verse comes from the **Greek** word **Kak-ee-ah**, found in key G2549 which means, badness that is depraved, (immoral or corrupt) or malignant (hateful or mean) this effects the character, moral development (ethic and principles) and nature of a person. This word normally translates into **malice** which has its root in our hearts. This kind of evil normally results in severe damage being inflicted on others through our words. Our speech and conversation is a, tell (tell) sign for the work of malice.

"Let no corrupt communication proceed out of your mouth, but that which is good to the use of edifying, that it may minister grace unto the hearers. And grieve not the Holy Spirit of God, whereby ye are sealed unto the day of redemption: Let all bitterness, and wrath, and anger, and clamor, and evil speaking, be put away from you, with all malice."

Ephesians 4:29-31

Corrupt communication is one of the manifestations connected to malice which has its origin in evil. Individuals who are challenged in the place of edifying others are often guilty of grieving the Holy Spirit. Those who struggle in the area of spiritual gifts often need deliverance from spirits of anger and rage. Proverbs 15:1 states, "A soft answer turns away wrath, but grievous words, stir up anger." Satan has aborted the destiny of countless people and caused numerous others to abandon the call and assignment of God upon their lives because they can't control their tongues. Remember the words of Jesus according to Matthew 12:37, our words will justify or substantiate, or condemn.

"But now ye also put off these: anger, wrath, malice, blasphemy, filthy communication out of your mouth."
Colossians 3:8

The Colossian believers were admonished to put off, discard, remove from their midst; anger, wrath, malice, blaspheming and filthy communication out of their mouths. Once again malice which translates into evil is connected to unclean communication. Profanity and all sorts of unwholesome conversation are the products of evil. Jesus declares the words I speak unto you they are spirit and they are life. God desires for us to speak life, yet Satan through our unredeemed nature has found a way to successfully amass momentum by causing man to speak his own demise. May your mouth be full of God's words and a life governed by His promises.

"Wherefore laying aside all malice, guile, and hypocrisies, and envies, and evil speaking, as newborn babes desire the sincere milk of the word, that ye may grow thereby."
I Peter 2:1-2

Once again we are encouraged to deal with malice in this reference by laying it aside. This verse brings yet another interesting connection to our speech and conversation because of malice. Hypocrisy and envy are mentioned in this verse. This leads to another manifestation which happens to be the product of malice. People who are hypocritical and manifests jealousy could possibly be in the snare of malice. A snare is something set as a trap. Satan has established all kinds of snares for the believer and nonbeliever alike. The word of the Lord declares we are ensnared by the words of our own mouth. As your desire for the sincerity of the word increases, malice will be overcome. Press into the Word!

Lord, deliver me from evil…

"Lord set a watch at my mouth and keep the door of my lips. Lord, guard me from all hypocrisy and envy. Deliver me from all unwholesome speaking and filthy communication. I renounce all negativity and bitterness in my heart. I ask you to heal me of any hurts and gaping wounds that would cause my mouth to spew out poison. I decree I am healed of the Lord and my conversation is undefiled in Jesus name amen!"

There are times in the natural when things we do appear to be innocent and pose no threat. However, we are admonished in **I Thessalonians 5:22-23 to** *"Abstain from all appearance of evil. And the very God of peace sanctify you wholly; and I pray God your whole spirit and soul and body be preserved blameless unto the coming of our Lord Jesus Christ."* Notice how abstaining from the appearance of evil gives access to peace, which sanctifies and preserves our entire being blameless. Sometimes what appears to be innocent can actually be evil. The reference for evil in this scripture is the *Greek word **poneros*** found in key **G4190.** It means hurtful, anguish or pain; e.g. the effect or influence on a person's life; this kind of evil results in bondage or injury; especially internal and/or emotional pain.

One example that can be used to describe how the appearance of evil can produce bondage or injury is dating. Listen carefully before you stone me. In our local church we have advised those who desire to date, to ask mature married couples to chaperone them. This provides a measure of safety and is also healthy because when individuals are chaperoned by mature married couples, they are able to witness a living example. We had an incident when our church first began where this standard was suggested to two individuals desiring to date. They refused to comply and their actions, though appearing innocent, actually harmed others who saw them pursuing one another apart from the standard set by our leadership. Rebellion to authority is always going to be an open invitation for evil. This act injured the two involved and also temporarily effected our congregation. Whether or not you have a visible position in your local church you should adhere to the standards set by leadership to ensure that what you do, though appearing innocent doesn't become evil.

"Blessed are ye, when men shall revile you and persecute you and shall say all manner of evil against you falsely, for my sake."
Matthew 5:11

Jesus states that we are blessed when men revile us; which means to insult, offend and be rude to. He also states that we are blessed when men persecute us; which means to harass, single out and discriminate against. The Lord further states "...man shall say all manner of evil against us falsely for his sake." This is interesting because the insults and harassment has nothing to do with us, but everything to do with Him. Serving the Lord requires a revelation of his suffering as well.

Satan however has been able to undermine many believers by singling us out and launching all kinds of assaults because of our commitment to righteousness. This is most often seen in households where one spouse is saved and the other is not. This is also prevalent in workplaces where one coworker is saved and the other is not.

We are to develop a healthy and personal relationship with Jesus, but we cannot allow the things spoken against us because of this relationship to detour us from pursuing him. Remember the Genesis of evil brought a separation between God and his creation. There is grace available for you to endure injustice for his sake. May grace be ministered unto you in abundance.

"The light of the body is the eye: if therefore thine eye be single, thy whole body shall be full of light. But if thine eye be evil, thy whole body shall be full of darkness. If therefore the light that is in thee be darkness, how great is that darkness!"

Matthew 6:22-23

The Lord is using once again a natural example to reveal a deeper spiritual truth. The eye in this verse speaks of a person's vision. This speaks of our ability to see and the mental pictures that are active in our imagination. It can also have to do with our perception. So our eyes illuminate our bodies, if our eyes or vision is evil because bondage or suffering from an injury due to anguish or pain our bodies or lifestyles become full of darkness.

The Lord declares that men loved darkness because their deeds are evil. People who have an evil eye will normally be used by Satan to cause injury and put others in bondage because of their twisted views and opinions. This is why we need to have the eyes of our understanding enlightened by God's word allowing Him to be the only source of enlightenment.

There are many people whose eyes have become evil because of incidents in their own lives where they received wounds and injuries from others. This is the catalyst that holds true to a statement I've heard on many occasions, hurt people hurt people. Take a few moments right now and ask the Lord to give you a single eye so that your body can be full of light!

Lord, deliver me from evil…

"Father I give you thanks for your goodness and your mercy towards me. You are so faithful to encourage me and strengthen me from your word. So I speak your word over my life and I declare I have single vision. My eyes and my heart are solely fixed upon you. I decree that all assignments of evil rooted in injuries, anguish and bondage are broken off of my destiny and purpose. I am in Christ, the Light of the world according to Matthew 5:14 and my light is shining bright and men see my good works, and glorify You in heaven. I proclaim this in the mighty name of Jesus. Amen!"

Chapter 4

The Root of All Evil

THE ROOT OF ALL EVIL

Our final thought on this subject of evil comes from the **Greek** word **Kakos** found in key G2556. It means to perish in your own corruption; this is rooted in selfishness, greed, covetousness and lust. Driving desire for forbidden things is the fruit of kakos type of evil. Believers who are bound by this kind of evil often find themselves being ruled by or involved in destructive behavior, relationships and situations.

I Timothy 6:10 states, *"For the love of money is the root of all evil: which while some coveted after, they have erred from the faith, and pierced themselves through with many sorrows."* I have often heard believers quote this verse and equate money in itself as being the source of evil. That is not what this verse is saying. Closer examination reveals that love for money is the root system which supports all kinds of evil. We are told to love God with all our heart, with all our soul and mind. From this perspective we can see how loving money or anything else in the place of loving God first will cause evil to manifest. When we allow desire to develop an appetite for selfish and covetous means we will soon perish in our own corruption.

"Moreover, brethren, I would not that you should be ignorant, how that all our fathers were under the cloud, and all pass through the sea; And were all baptized unto Moses in the cloud and in the sea; And did all eat the same

spiritual meat; And did all drink the same spiritual drink: for they drank of that spiritual Rock that followed them: and that Rock was Christ. But with many of them God was not well pleased: for they were overthrown in the wilderness. Now these things were our examples, to the intent that we should not lust after evil things, as they also lusted."

I Corinthians 10:1-6

The Corinthian believers were very gifted and equally carnal. The apostle Paul was admonishing them from a historical example concerning the children of Israel. God was provoked to displeasure with the Israelites because of their desire for forbidden things. In other words their selfishness, greed and lust angered the Lord. They worshiped idols, practiced fornication; tempted Christ and murmured often.

> *The Spirit of God will help us to temper our appetites and desires as we study the word of God, fast and pray.*

The Corinthian believers were headed down the same path and the apostle Paul was warning them to not continue because just like God dealt with Israel, he was going to do with them. We must guard our hearts from any individuals and objects that demand more of our attention than God Himself. The Spirit of God will help us to temper our appetites and desires as we study the word of God, fast and pray. These three disciplines are vital for the believer and have been proven to help overcome evil, its influences and its effects.

I pray that this teaching has empowered you to discern evil and encouraged you to cry unto the Lord for deliverance in a greater way. I declare deliverance and breakthrough over your life from all assignments of darkness bent on fostering your destruction. May a fresh anointing for spiritual warfare and deliverance come on you mightily I pray.

Lord, deliver me from evil…

"Father I thank you for opening my eyes and causing me to rightfully discern between that which is good and evil. I ask you to cultivate a desire for you above all else. I trust you and I yield to your Spirit. He leads and guides me into all truth. Thank you Lord for being so faithful and consistent in helping me to truly be delivered from evil, in Jesus name Amen!"

More Great Resources from Stephen A. Garner Ministries

Books
- Apostolic Pioneering
- Benefits of Praying in Tongues
- Exposing the Spirit of Anger
- Fundamentals of Deliverance 101, Revised & Expanded
- Ministering Spirits: "Engaging the Angelic Realm"
- Essentials of the Prophetic Revised & Expanded
- Pray Without Ceasing, Special Edition
- Restoring Prophetic Watchmen
- Kingdom Prayer
- The Kingdom of God: A Believer's Guide to Kingdom Living
- Prayers, Decrees and Confessions for Wisdom
- Prayers, Decrees and Confessions for Favour & Grace
- Prayers, Decrees and Confessions for Prosperity
- Prayers, Decrees and Confessions for Increase
- Prayers, Decrees and Confessions for Righteousness, Revised & Expanded
- Prayers, Decrees and Confessions for Goodness & Mercy
- Prayers, Decrees and Confessions for Power
- Prayers the Strengthen Marriages and Families

CD's
- Prayers for the Nations
- Prayers Against Python & Witchcraft
- Prayers of Healing & Restoration
- Prayers of Renunciation and Deliverance
- Thy Kingdom Come
- Latter Rain
- Overcoming Spirits of Terrorism
- Songs of Intercession
- The Spirit of the Breaker
- The Fear of the Lord

CONTACT INFORMATION
STEPHEN A. GARNER MINISTRIES
P.O. BOX 1545, BOLINGBROOK, IL 60440
EMAIL: SAGARNERMINISTRIES@GMAIL.COM
WWW.SAGMINISTRIES.COM

www.ingramcontent.com/pod-product-compliance
Lightning Source LLC
LaVergne TN
LVHW051205080426
835508LV00021B/2820